Twin Care

Laura Rizer

IISBN-13: 978-1724708045

ISBN-10: 172470804X

"I don't know how you did it. I'm overwhelmed with just one!"

When my twins were babies, this is what I often heard when I met other new moms. And to be completely honest, looking back 4 years later, sometimes I am not sure myself. Being a first time mother to two babies at the same time is exhausting, draining, and frankly scary. But was also amazing, empowering, and I wouldn't trade it for any other experience in the world.

Now that I find myself in the role of "experienced twin mom" I'm so happy that I can take a few of the lessons that I learned with my twins to help keep my friends from becoming overwhelmed. I've shared my #1 secret with them, and now I'm sharing it with you too.

KEEPING A DAILY BABY CARE LOG

When you have twins, it's more important than ever to get organized. It's the way I keep from becoming overwhelmed and overstressed when it comes to life with two babies (then two toddlers...).

When my twins were babies, keeping a daily baby log was an absolute necessity. A daily baby log will help you to keep a record of your baby's care and to help you keep things straight in the exhausting early days, weeks, and even months of parenthood. The baby care log is perfect for moms, caregivers, and even makes a great gift.

This baby care journal will help you track baby's day and makes a great record for you to share with doctors or other caregivers. I remember when my boys were tiny and our doctor would ask how much they were eating, how many diapers they were going through, etc. My sleep deprived brain was so fogged (and I was keeping track of two) that it was so awesome to just hand her my log sheets and know I was giving her the right information. And it's a fun record to go back and look through (I just peeked through ours again).

The twin baby care journal includes spaces to record:

- Feeding Times & Amounts. There is space for both breast and bottle feeding (I did both). And lots of spaces - twins eat often!
- Diaper Changes. Simply check "wet" or "dirty" to keep a running count.
- Sleep & Nap Times. Track the start and end times of baby's naps and sleep.
- Tummy Time. Include the start and end time (I had one baby that hated tummy time and one that loved it).
- Medications. Keep a record of medication, dosage, and time given.
- Notes. A fun place to record any milestones or things you want to remember.

You'll have enough pages to record 3 months of days with one page per baby. Simply write each twin's name at the top and record their care each day.

And remember mama, you've got this.

NAME: _____ DATE: _____

FEEDING

Time	Breast (Time) L / R	Bottle (oz.)

DIAPERS

Wet	Dirty
☐	☐
☐	☐
☐	☐
☐	☐
☐	☐
☐	☐
☐	☐
☐	☐

TUMMY TIME

Start Time	End Time

SLEEP/NAPS

Start Time	End Time

MEDICATIONS

Time	Name & Dosage

NOTES

NAME: _____   DATE: _____

FEEDING

Time	Breast (Time)	L / R	Bottle (oz.)

DIAPERS

Wet	Dirty
☐	☐
☐	☐
☐	☐
☐	☐
☐	☐
☐	☐
☐	☐

TUMMY TIME

Start Time	End Time

SLEEP/NAPS

Start Time	End Time

MEDICATIONS

Time	Name & Dosage

NOTES

NAME: _____   DATE: _____

FEEDING

Time	Breast (Time)	L / R	Bottle (oz.)

DIAPERS

Wet	Dirty
☐	☐
☐	☐
☐	☐
☐	☐
☐	☐
☐	☐
☐	☐

TUMMY TIME

Start Time	End Time

SLEEP/NAPS

Start Time	End Time

MEDICATIONS

Time	Name & Dosage

NOTES

NAME: _____ DATE: _____

FEEDING

Time	Breast (Time)	L / R	Bottle (oz.)

DIAPERS

Wet	Dirty
☐	☐
☐	☐
☐	☐
☐	☐
☐	☐
☐	☐
☐	☐

TUMMY TIME

Start Time	End Time

SLEEP/NAPS

Start Time	End Time

MEDICATIONS

Time	Name & Dosage

NOTES

NAME: _____ DATE: _____

FEEDING

Time	Breast (Time)	L / R	Bottle (oz.)

DIAPERS

Wet	Dirty
☐	☐
☐	☐
☐	☐
☐	☐
☐	☐
☐	☐
☐	☐
☐	☐

TUMMY TIME

Start Time	End Time

SLEEP/NAPS

Start Time	End Time

MEDICATIONS

Time	Name & Dosage

NOTES

NAME: _____ DATE: _____

FEEDING

Time	Breast (Time)	L / R	Bottle (oz.)

DIAPERS

Wet	Dirty
☐	☐
☐	☐
☐	☐
☐	☐
☐	☐
☐	☐
☐	☐
☐	☐

TUMMY TIME

Start Time	End Time

SLEEP/NAPS

Start Time	End Time

MEDICATIONS

Time	Name & Dosage

NOTES

NAME: _____   DATE: _____

FEEDING

TIME	BREAST (TIME)	L / R	BOTTLE (OZ.)

DIAPERS

WET	DIRTY
☐	☐
☐	☐
☐	☐
☐	☐
☐	☐
☐	☐
☐	☐
☐	☐

TUMMY TIME

START TIME	END TIME

SLEEP/NAPS

START TIME	END TIME

MEDICATIONS

TIME	NAME & DOSAGE

NOTES

NAME: _____   DATE: _____

FEEDING

Time	Breast (Time)	L / R	Bottle (oz.)

DIAPERS

Wet	Dirty
☐	☐
☐	☐
☐	☐
☐	☐
☐	☐
☐	☐
☐	☐

TUMMY TIME

Start Time	End Time

SLEEP/NAPS

Start Time	End Time

MEDICATIONS

Time	Name & Dosage

NOTES

NAME: _____ DATE: _____

FEEDING

TIME	BREAST (TIME)	L / R	BOTTLE (OZ.)

DIAPERS

WET	DIRTY

TUMMY TIME

START TIME	END TIME

SLEEP/NAPS

START TIME	END TIME

MEDICATIONS

TIME	NAME & DOSAGE

NOTES

NAME: _____ DATE: _____

FEEDING

Time	Breast (Time)	L / R	Bottle (oz.)

DIAPERS

Wet	Dirty
☐	☐
☐	☐
☐	☐
☐	☐
☐	☐
☐	☐
☐	☐
☐	☐

TUMMY TIME

Start Time	End Time

SLEEP/NAPS

Start Time	End Time

MEDICATIONS

Time	Name & Dosage

NOTES

NAME: _____ DATE: _____

FEEDING

TIME	BREAST (TIME) L / R	BOTTLE (OZ.)

DIAPERS

WET	DIRTY
☐	☐
☐	☐
☐	☐
☐	☐
☐	☐
☐	☐
☐	☐
☐	☐

TUMMY TIME

START TIME	END TIME

SLEEP/NAPS

START TIME	END TIME

MEDICATIONS

TIME	NAME & DOSAGE

NOTES

NAME: _____   DATE: _____

FEEDING

Time	Breast (Time)	L / R	Bottle (oz.)

DIAPERS

Wet	Dirty
☐	☐
☐	☐
☐	☐
☐	☐
☐	☐
☐	☐
☐	☐

TUMMY TIME

Start Time	End Time

SLEEP/NAPS

Start Time	End Time

MEDICATIONS

Time	Name & Dosage

NOTES

NAME: _____ DATE: _____

FEEDING

Time	Breast (Time)	L / R	Bottle (oz.)

DIAPERS

Wet	Dirty
☐	☐
☐	☐
☐	☐
☐	☐
☐	☐
☐	☐
☐	☐
☐	☐

TUMMY TIME

Start Time	End Time

SLEEP/NAPS

Start Time	End Time

MEDICATIONS

Time	Name & Dosage

NOTES

NAME: _____ DATE: _____

FEEDING

Time	Breast (Time)	L / R	Bottle (oz.)

DIAPERS

Wet	Dirty
☐	☐
☐	☐
☐	☐
☐	☐
☐	☐
☐	☐
☐	☐

TUMMY TIME

Start Time	End Time

SLEEP/NAPS

Start Time	End Time

MEDICATIONS

Time	Name & Dosage

NOTES

NAME: _____   DATE: _____

FEEDING

Time	Breast (Time) L / R	Bottle (oz.)

DIAPERS

Wet	Dirty
☐	☐
☐	☐
☐	☐
☐	☐
☐	☐
☐	☐
☐	☐
☐	☐

TUMMY TIME

Start Time	End Time

SLEEP/NAPS

Start Time	End Time

MEDICATIONS

Time	Name & Dosage

NOTES

NAME: _____   DATE: _____

FEEDING

Time	Breast (Time)	L / R	Bottle (oz.)

DIAPERS

Wet	Dirty
☐	☐
☐	☐
☐	☐
☐	☐
☐	☐
☐	☐
☐	☐

TUMMY TIME

Start Time	End Time

SLEEP/NAPS

Start Time	End Time

MEDICATIONS

Time	Name & Dosage

NOTES

NAME: _____ DATE: _____

FEEDING

TIME	BREAST (TIME)	L / R	BOTTLE (OZ.)

DIAPERS

Wet	Dirty
☐	☐
☐	☐
☐	☐
☐	☐
☐	☐
☐	☐
☐	☐

TUMMY TIME

START TIME	END TIME

SLEEP/NAPS

START TIME	END TIME

MEDICATIONS

TIME	NAME & DOSAGE

NOTES

NAME: _____   DATE: _____

FEEDING

Time	Breast (Time)	L / R	Bottle (oz.)

DIAPERS

Wet	Dirty
☐	☐
☐	☐
☐	☐
☐	☐
☐	☐
☐	☐
☐	☐

TUMMY TIME

Start Time	End Time

SLEEP/NAPS

Start Time	End Time

MEDICATIONS

Time	Name & Dosage

NOTES

NAME: _____   DATE: _____

FEEDING

TIME	BREAST (TIME)	L / R	BOTTLE (OZ.)

DIAPERS

WET	DIRTY
☐	☐
☐	☐
☐	☐
☐	☐
☐	☐
☐	☐
☐	☐
☐	☐

TUMMY TIME

START TIME	END TIME

SLEEP/NAPS

START TIME	END TIME

MEDICATIONS

TIME	NAME & DOSAGE

NOTES

NAME: _____ DATE: _____

FEEDING

Time	Breast (Time)	L / R	Bottle (oz.)

DIAPERS

Wet	Dirty
☐	☐
☐	☐
☐	☐
☐	☐
☐	☐
☐	☐
☐	☐
☐	☐

TUMMY TIME

Start Time	End Time

SLEEP/NAPS

Start Time	End Time

MEDICATIONS

Time	Name & Dosage

NOTES

NAME: _____   DATE: _____

FEEDING

Time	Breast (Time)	L / R	Bottle (oz.)

DIAPERS

Wet	Dirty

TUMMY TIME

Start Time	End Time

SLEEP/NAPS

Start Time	End Time

MEDICATIONS

Time	Name & Dosage

NOTES

NAME: _____ DATE: _____

FEEDING

TIME	BREAST (TIME)	L / R	BOTTLE (OZ.)

DIAPERS

WET	DIRTY
☐	☐
☐	☐
☐	☐
☐	☐
☐	☐
☐	☐
☐	☐
☐	☐

TUMMY TIME

START TIME	END TIME

SLEEP/NAPS

START TIME	END TIME

MEDICATIONS

TIME	NAME & DOSAGE

NOTES

NAME: _____ DATE: _____

FEEDING

Time	Breast (Time)	L / R	Bottle (oz.)

DIAPERS

Wet	Dirty
☐	☐
☐	☐
☐	☐
☐	☐
☐	☐
☐	☐
☐	☐

TUMMY TIME

Start Time	End Time

SLEEP/NAPS

Start Time	End Time

MEDICATIONS

Time	Name & Dosage

NOTES

NAME: _____   DATE: _____

FEEDING

TIME	BREAST (TIME)	L / R	BOTTLE (OZ.)

DIAPERS

WET	DIRTY
☐	☐
☐	☐
☐	☐
☐	☐
☐	☐
☐	☐
☐	☐

TUMMY TIME

START TIME	END TIME

SLEEP/NAPS

START TIME	END TIME

MEDICATIONS

TIME	NAME & DOSAGE

NOTES

NAME: _____   DATE: _____

FEEDING

Time	Breast (Time)	L / R	Bottle (oz.)

DIAPERS

Wet	Dirty
☐	☐
☐	☐
☐	☐
☐	☐
☐	☐
☐	☐
☐	☐
☐	☐

TUMMY TIME

Start Time	End Time

SLEEP/NAPS

Start Time	End Time

MEDICATIONS

Time	Name & Dosage

NOTES

NAME: _____ DATE: _____

FEEDING

Time	Breast (Time) L / R		Bottle (oz.)

DIAPERS

Wet	Dirty
☐	☐
☐	☐
☐	☐
☐	☐
☐	☐
☐	☐
☐	☐
☐	☐

TUMMY TIME

Start Time	End Time

SLEEP/NAPS

Start Time	End Time

MEDICATIONS

Time	Name & Dosage

NOTES

NAME: _____   DATE: _____

FEEDING

TIME	BREAST (TIME)	L / R	BOTTLE (OZ.)

DIAPERS

WET	DIRTY
☐	☐
☐	☐
☐	☐
☐	☐
☐	☐
☐	☐
☐	☐
☐	☐

TUMMY TIME

START TIME	END TIME

SLEEP/NAPS

START TIME	END TIME

MEDICATIONS

TIME	NAME & DOSAGE

NOTES

NAME: _____   DATE: _____

FEEDING

Time	Breast (Time)	L / R	Bottle (Oz.)

DIAPERS

Wet	Dirty
☐	☐
☐	☐
☐	☐
☐	☐
☐	☐
☐	☐
☐	☐
☐	☐

TUMMY TIME

Start Time	End Time

SLEEP/NAPS

Start Time	End Time

MEDICATIONS

Time	Name & Dosage

NOTES

NAME: _____ DATE: _____

FEEDING

Time	Breast (Time)	L / R	Bottle (oz.)

DIAPERS

Wet	Dirty
☐	☐
☐	☐
☐	☐
☐	☐
☐	☐
☐	☐
☐	☐
☐	☐

TUMMY TIME

Start Time	End Time

SLEEP/NAPS

Start Time	End Time

MEDICATIONS

Time	Name & Dosage

NOTES

NAME: _____   DATE: _____

FEEDING

Time	Breast (Time)	L / R	Bottle (oz.)

DIAPERS

Wet	Dirty
☐	☐
☐	☐
☐	☐
☐	☐
☐	☐
☐	☐
☐	☐
☐	☐

TUMMY TIME

Start Time	End Time

SLEEP/NAPS

Start Time	End Time

MEDICATIONS

Time	Name & Dosage

NOTES

NAME: _____   DATE: _____

FEEDING

TIME	BREAST (TIME)	L / R	BOTTLE (OZ.)

DIAPERS

WET	DIRTY
☐	☐
☐	☐
☐	☐
☐	☐
☐	☐
☐	☐
☐	☐

TUMMY TIME

START TIME	END TIME

SLEEP/NAPS

START TIME	END TIME

MEDICATIONS

TIME	NAME & DOSAGE

NOTES

NAME: _____ DATE: _____

FEEDING

Time	Breast (Time)	L / R	Bottle (oz.)

DIAPERS

Wet	Dirty
☐	☐
☐	☐
☐	☐
☐	☐
☐	☐
☐	☐
☐	☐
☐	☐

TUMMY TIME

Start Time	End Time

SLEEP/NAPS

Start Time	End Time

MEDICATIONS

Time	Name & Dosage

NOTES

NAME: _____ DATE: _____

FEEDING

TIME	BREAST (TIME)	L / R	BOTTLE (OZ.)

DIAPERS

WET	DIRTY

TUMMY TIME

START TIME	END TIME

SLEEP/NAPS

START TIME	END TIME

MEDICATIONS

TIME	NAME & DOSAGE

NOTES

NAME: _____   DATE: _____

FEEDING

Time	Breast (Time)	L / R	Bottle (oz.)

DIAPERS

Wet	Dirty
☐	☐
☐	☐
☐	☐
☐	☐
☐	☐
☐	☐
☐	☐
☐	☐

TUMMY TIME

Start Time	End Time

SLEEP/NAPS

Start Time	End Time

MEDICATIONS

Time	Name & Dosage

NOTES

NAME: _____   DATE: _____

FEEDING

TIME	BREAST (TIME)	L / R	BOTTLE (OZ.)

DIAPERS

WET	DIRTY
☐	☐
☐	☐
☐	☐
☐	☐
☐	☐
☐	☐
☐	☐
☐	☐

TUMMY TIME

START TIME	END TIME

SLEEP/NAPS

START TIME	END TIME

MEDICATIONS

TIME	NAME & DOSAGE

NOTES

NAME: _____   DATE: _____

FEEDING

TIME	BREAST (TIME)	L / R	BOTTLE (OZ.)

DIAPERS

WET	DIRTY

TUMMY TIME

START TIME	END TIME

SLEEP/NAPS

START TIME	END TIME

MEDICATIONS

TIME	NAME & DOSAGE

NOTES

NAME: _____   DATE: _____

FEEDING

Time	Breast (Time)	L / R	Bottle (oz.)

DIAPERS

Wet	Dirty
☐	☐
☐	☐
☐	☐
☐	☐
☐	☐
☐	☐
☐	☐

TUMMY TIME

Start Time	End Time

SLEEP/NAPS

Start Time	End Time

MEDICATIONS

Time	Name & Dosage

NOTES

NAME: _____   DATE: _____

FEEDING

Time	Breast (Time)	L / R	Bottle (oz.)

DIAPERS

Wet	Dirty
☐	☐
☐	☐
☐	☐
☐	☐
☐	☐
☐	☐
☐	☐

TUMMY TIME

Start Time	End Time

SLEEP/NAPS

Start Time	End Time

MEDICATIONS

Time	Name & Dosage

NOTES

NAME: _____ DATE: _____

FEEDING

TIME	BREAST (TIME)	L / R	BOTTLE (OZ.)

DIAPERS

WET	DIRTY
☐	☐
☐	☐
☐	☐
☐	☐
☐	☐
☐	☐
☐	☐

TUMMY TIME

START TIME	END TIME

SLEEP/NAPS

START TIME	END TIME

MEDICATIONS

TIME	NAME & DOSAGE

NOTES

NAME: _____   DATE: _____

FEEDING

Time	Breast (Time)	L / R	Bottle (oz.)

DIAPERS

Wet	Dirty
☐	☐
☐	☐
☐	☐
☐	☐
☐	☐
☐	☐
☐	☐
☐	☐

TUMMY TIME

Start Time	End Time

SLEEP/NAPS

Start Time	End Time

MEDICATIONS

Time	Name & Dosage

NOTES

NAME: _____   DATE: _____

FEEDING

Time	Breast (Time)	L / R	Bottle (oz.)

DIAPERS

Wet	Dirty
☐	☐
☐	☐
☐	☐
☐	☐
☐	☐
☐	☐
☐	☐
☐	☐

TUMMY TIME

Start Time	End Time

SLEEP/NAPS

Start Time	End Time

MEDICATIONS

Time	Name & Dosage

NOTES

NAME: _____ DATE: _____

FEEDING

Time	Breast (Time)	L / R	Bottle (oz.)

DIAPERS

Wet	Dirty
☐	☐
☐	☐
☐	☐
☐	☐
☐	☐
☐	☐
☐	☐

TUMMY TIME

Start Time	End Time

SLEEP/NAPS

Start Time	End Time

MEDICATIONS

Time	Name & Dosage

NOTES

NAME: _____ DATE: _____

FEEDING

Time	Breast (Time)	L / R	Bottle (oz.)

DIAPERS

Wet	Dirty
☐	☐
☐	☐
☐	☐
☐	☐
☐	☐
☐	☐
☐	☐

TUMMY TIME

Start Time	End Time

SLEEP/NAPS

Start Time	End Time

MEDICATIONS

Time	Name & Dosage

NOTES

NAME: _____   DATE: _____

FEEDING

Time	Breast (Time)	L / R	Bottle (oz.)

DIAPERS

Wet	Dirty
☐	☐
☐	☐
☐	☐
☐	☐
☐	☐
☐	☐
☐	☐

TUMMY TIME

Start Time	End Time

SLEEP/NAPS

Start Time	End Time

MEDICATIONS

Time	Name & Dosage

NOTES

NAME: _____ DATE: _____

FEEDING

Time	Breast (Time)	L / R	Bottle (oz.)

DIAPERS

Wet	Dirty
☐	☐
☐	☐
☐	☐
☐	☐
☐	☐
☐	☐
☐	☐
☐	☐

TUMMY TIME

Start Time	End Time

SLEEP/NAPS

Start Time	End Time

MEDICATIONS

Time	Name & Dosage

NOTES

NAME: _____   DATE: _____

FEEDING

Time	Breast (Time) L / R	Bottle (oz.)

DIAPERS

Wet	Dirty
☐	☐
☐	☐
☐	☐
☐	☐
☐	☐
☐	☐
☐	☐

TUMMY TIME

Start Time	End Time

SLEEP/NAPS

Start Time	End Time

MEDICATIONS

Time	Name & Dosage

NOTES

NAME: _____   DATE: _____

FEEDING

TIME	BREAST (TIME)	L / R	BOTTLE (OZ.)

DIAPERS

WET	DIRTY
☐	☐
☐	☐
☐	☐
☐	☐
☐	☐
☐	☐
☐	☐
☐	☐

TUMMY TIME

START TIME	END TIME

SLEEP/NAPS

START TIME	END TIME

MEDICATIONS

TIME	NAME & DOSAGE

NOTES

NAME: _____ DATE: _____

FEEDING

Time	Breast (Time) L / R	Bottle (oz.)

DIAPERS

Wet	Dirty
☐	☐
☐	☐
☐	☐
☐	☐
☐	☐
☐	☐
☐	☐
☐	☐

TUMMY TIME

Start Time	End Time

SLEEP/NAPS

Start Time	End Time

MEDICATIONS

Time	Name & Dosage

NOTES

NAME: _____   DATE: _____

FEEDING

TIME	BREAST (TIME)	L / R	BOTTLE (OZ.)

DIAPERS

WET	DIRTY
☐	☐
☐	☐
☐	☐
☐	☐
☐	☐
☐	☐
☐	☐

TUMMY TIME

START TIME	END TIME

SLEEP/NAPS

START TIME	END TIME

MEDICATIONS

TIME	NAME & DOSAGE

NOTES

NAME: _____ DATE: _____

FEEDING

Time	Breast (Time) L / R	Bottle (oz.)

DIAPERS

Wet	Dirty
☐	☐
☐	☐
☐	☐
☐	☐
☐	☐
☐	☐
☐	☐
☐	☐

TUMMY TIME

Start Time	End Time

SLEEP/NAPS

Start Time	End Time

MEDICATIONS

Time	Name & Dosage

NOTES

NAME: _____   DATE: _____

FEEDING

Time	Breast (Time)	L / R	Bottle (Oz.)

DIAPERS

Wet	Dirty

TUMMY TIME

Start Time	End Time

SLEEP/NAPS

Start Time	End Time

MEDICATIONS

Time	Name & Dosage

NOTES

NAME: _____   DATE: _____

FEEDING

Time	Breast (Time) L / R	Bottle (oz.)

DIAPERS

Wet	Dirty
☐	☐
☐	☐
☐	☐
☐	☐
☐	☐
☐	☐
☐	☐
☐	☐

TUMMY TIME

Start Time	End Time

SLEEP/NAPS

Start Time	End Time

MEDICATIONS

Time	Name & Dosage

NOTES

NAME: _____   DATE: _____

FEEDING

Time	Breast (Time)	L / R	Bottle (oz.)

DIAPERS

Wet	Dirty
☐	☐
☐	☐
☐	☐
☐	☐
☐	☐
☐	☐
☐	☐

TUMMY TIME

Start Time	End Time

SLEEP/NAPS

Start Time	End Time

MEDICATIONS

Time	Name & Dosage

NOTES

NAME: _____ DATE: _____

FEEDING

Time	Breast (Time)	L / R	Bottle (oz.)

DIAPERS

Wet	Dirty
☐	☐
☐	☐
☐	☐
☐	☐
☐	☐
☐	☐
☐	☐
☐	☐

TUMMY TIME

Start Time	End Time

SLEEP/NAPS

Start Time	End Time

MEDICATIONS

Time	Name & Dosage

NOTES

NAME: _____ DATE: _____

FEEDING

Time	Breast (Time)	L / R	Bottle (oz.)

DIAPERS

Wet	Dirty
☐	☐
☐	☐
☐	☐
☐	☐
☐	☐
☐	☐
☐	☐

TUMMY TIME

Start Time	End Time

SLEEP/NAPS

Start Time	End Time

MEDICATIONS

Time	Name & Dosage

NOTES

NAME: _____ DATE: _____

FEEDING

Time	Breast (Time)	L / R	Bottle (oz.)

DIAPERS

Wet	Dirty

TUMMY TIME

Start Time	End Time

SLEEP/NAPS

Start Time	End Time

MEDICATIONS

Time	Name & Dosage

NOTES

NAME: _____   DATE: _____

FEEDING

TIME	BREAST (TIME)	L / R	BOTTLE (OZ.)

DIAPERS

WET	DIRTY
☐	☐
☐	☐
☐	☐
☐	☐
☐	☐
☐	☐
☐	☐
☐	☐

TUMMY TIME

START TIME	END TIME

SLEEP/NAPS

START TIME	END TIME

MEDICATIONS

TIME	NAME & DOSAGE

NOTES

NAME: _____   DATE: _____

FEEDING

TIME	BREAST (TIME)	L / R	BOTTLE (OZ.)

DIAPERS

WET	DIRTY

TUMMY TIME

START TIME	END TIME

SLEEP/NAPS

START TIME	END TIME

MEDICATIONS

TIME	NAME & DOSAGE

NOTES

NAME: _____   DATE: _____

FEEDING

TIME	BREAST (TIME)	L / R	BOTTLE (OZ.)

DIAPERS

WET	DIRTY

TUMMY TIME

START TIME	END TIME

SLEEP/NAPS

START TIME	END TIME

MEDICATIONS

TIME	NAME & DOSAGE

NOTES

NAME: _____ DATE: _____

FEEDING

TIME	BREAST (TIME) L / R	BOTTLE (OZ.)

DIAPERS

WET	DIRTY
☐	☐
☐	☐
☐	☐
☐	☐
☐	☐
☐	☐
☐	☐
☐	☐

TUMMY TIME

START TIME	END TIME

SLEEP/NAPS

START TIME	END TIME

MEDICATIONS

TIME	NAME & DOSAGE

NOTES

NAME: _____   DATE: _____

FEEDING

TIME	BREAST (TIME)	L / R	BOTTLE (OZ.)

DIAPERS

WET	DIRTY
☐	☐
☐	☐
☐	☐
☐	☐
☐	☐
☐	☐
☐	☐
☐	☐

TUMMY TIME

START TIME	END TIME

SLEEP/NAPS

START TIME	END TIME

MEDICATIONS

TIME	NAME & DOSAGE

NOTES

NAME: _____ DATE: _____

FEEDING

Time	Breast (Time)	L / R	Bottle (oz.)

DIAPERS

Wet	Dirty
☐	☐
☐	☐
☐	☐
☐	☐
☐	☐
☐	☐
☐	☐
☐	☐

TUMMY TIME

Start Time	End Time

SLEEP/NAPS

Start Time	End Time

MEDICATIONS

Time	Name & Dosage

NOTES

NAME: _____   DATE: _____

FEEDING

Time	Breast (Time)	L / R	Bottle (Oz.)

DIAPERS

Wet	Dirty
☐	☐
☐	☐
☐	☐
☐	☐
☐	☐
☐	☐
☐	☐
☐	☐

TUMMY TIME

Start Time	End Time

SLEEP/NAPS

Start Time	End Time

MEDICATIONS

Time	Name & Dosage

NOTES

NAME: _____   DATE: _____

FEEDING

Time	Breast (Time) L / R	Bottle (oz.)

DIAPERS

Wet	Dirty
☐	☐
☐	☐
☐	☐
☐	☐
☐	☐
☐	☐
☐	☐
☐	☐
☐	☐

TUMMY TIME

Start Time	End Time

SLEEP/NAPS

Start Time	End Time

MEDICATIONS

Time	Name & Dosage

NOTES

NAME: _____ DATE: _____

FEEDING

TIME	BREAST (TIME)	L / R	BOTTLE (OZ.)

DIAPERS

WET	DIRTY

TUMMY TIME

START TIME	END TIME

SLEEP/NAPS

START TIME	END TIME

MEDICATIONS

TIME	NAME & DOSAGE

NOTES

NAME: _____   DATE: _____

FEEDING

TIME	BREAST (TIME) L / R	BOTTLE (OZ.)

DIAPERS

WET	DIRTY
☐	☐
☐	☐
☐	☐
☐	☐
☐	☐
☐	☐
☐	☐
☐	☐

TUMMY TIME

START TIME	END TIME

SLEEP/NAPS

START TIME	END TIME

MEDICATIONS

TIME	NAME & DOSAGE

NOTES

NAME: _____ DATE: _____

FEEDING

Time	Breast (Time)	L / R	Bottle (oz.)

DIAPERS

Wet	Dirty
☐	☐
☐	☐
☐	☐
☐	☐
☐	☐
☐	☐
☐	☐
☐	☐

TUMMY TIME

Start Time	End Time

SLEEP/NAPS

Start Time	End Time

MEDICATIONS

Time	Name & Dosage

NOTES

NAME: _____ DATE: _____

FEEDING

Time	Breast (Time)	L / R	Bottle (oz.)

DIAPERS

Wet	Dirty
☐	☐
☐	☐
☐	☐
☐	☐
☐	☐
☐	☐
☐	☐
☐	☐

TUMMY TIME

Start Time	End Time

SLEEP/NAPS

Start Time	End Time

MEDICATIONS

Time	Name & Dosage

NOTES

NAME: _____   DATE: _____

FEEDING

Time	Breast (Time)	L / R	Bottle (oz.)

DIAPERS

Wet	Dirty
☐	☐
☐	☐
☐	☐
☐	☐
☐	☐
☐	☐
☐	☐

TUMMY TIME

Start Time	End Time

SLEEP/NAPS

Start Time	End Time

MEDICATIONS

Time	Name & Dosage

NOTES

NAME: _____   DATE: _____

FEEDING

Time	Breast (Time) L / R	Bottle (oz.)

DIAPERS

Wet	Dirty
☐	☐
☐	☐
☐	☐
☐	☐
☐	☐
☐	☐
☐	☐
☐	☐

TUMMY TIME

Start Time	End Time

SLEEP/NAPS

Start Time	End Time

MEDICATIONS

Time	Name & Dosage

NOTES

NAME: _____ DATE: _____

FEEDING

Time	Breast (Time) L / R	Bottle (oz.)

DIAPERS

Wet	Dirty
☐	☐
☐	☐
☐	☐
☐	☐
☐	☐
☐	☐
☐	☐
☐	☐

TUMMY TIME

Start Time	End Time

SLEEP/NAPS

Start Time	End Time

MEDICATIONS

Time	Name & Dosage

NOTES

NAME: _____   DATE: _____

FEEDING

TIME	BREAST (TIME)	L / R	BOTTLE (OZ.)

DIAPERS

WET	DIRTY

TUMMY TIME

START TIME	END TIME

SLEEP/NAPS

START TIME	END TIME

MEDICATIONS

TIME	NAME & DOSAGE

NOTES

NAME: _____   DATE: _____

FEEDING

TIME	BREAST (TIME)	L / R	BOTTLE (OZ.)

DIAPERS

WET	DIRTY

TUMMY TIME

START TIME	END TIME

SLEEP/NAPS

START TIME	END TIME

MEDICATIONS

TIME	NAME & DOSAGE

NOTES

NAME: _____ DATE: _____

FEEDING

Time	Breast (Time)	L / R	Bottle (oz.)

DIAPERS

Wet	Dirty
☐	☐
☐	☐
☐	☐
☐	☐
☐	☐
☐	☐
☐	☐
☐	☐

TUMMY TIME

Start Time	End Time

SLEEP/NAPS

Start Time	End Time

MEDICATIONS

Time	Name & Dosage

NOTES

NAME: _____ DATE: _____

FEEDING

TIME	BREAST (TIME) L / R	BOTTLE (OZ.)

DIAPERS

WET	DIRTY
☐	☐
☐	☐
☐	☐
☐	☐
☐	☐
☐	☐
☐	☐

TUMMY TIME

START TIME	END TIME

SLEEP/NAPS

START TIME	END TIME

MEDICATIONS

TIME	NAME & DOSAGE

NOTES

NAME: _____ DATE: _____

FEEDING

Time	Breast (Time)	L / R	Bottle (oz.)

DIAPERS

Wet	Dirty
☐	☐
☐	☐
☐	☐
☐	☐
☐	☐
☐	☐
☐	☐

TUMMY TIME

Start Time	End Time

SLEEP/NAPS

Start Time	End Time

MEDICATIONS

Time	Name & Dosage

NOTES

NAME: _____ DATE: _____

FEEDING

Time	Breast (Time)	L / R	Bottle (oz.)

DIAPERS

Wet	Dirty
☐	☐
☐	☐
☐	☐
☐	☐
☐	☐
☐	☐
☐	☐
☐	☐

TUMMY TIME

Start Time	End Time

SLEEP/NAPS

Start Time	End Time

MEDICATIONS

Time	Name & Dosage

NOTES

Name: _____ Date: _____

FEEDING

Time	Breast (Time) L / R	Bottle (oz.)

DIAPERS

Wet	Dirty
☐	☐
☐	☐
☐	☐
☐	☐
☐	☐
☐	☐
☐	☐
☐	☐

TUMMY TIME

Start Time	End Time

SLEEP/NAPS

Start Time	End Time

MEDICATIONS

Time	Name & Dosage

NOTES

NAME: _____ DATE: _____

FEEDING

Time	Breast (Time)	L / R	Bottle (Oz.)

DIAPERS

Wet	Dirty
☐	☐
☐	☐
☐	☐
☐	☐
☐	☐
☐	☐
☐	☐
☐	☐

TUMMY TIME

Start Time	End Time

SLEEP/NAPS

Start Time	End Time

MEDICATIONS

Time	Name & Dosage

NOTES

NAME: _____   DATE: _____

FEEDING

Time	Breast (Time)	L / R	Bottle (oz.)

DIAPERS

Wet	Dirty

TUMMY TIME

Start Time	End Time

SLEEP/NAPS

Start Time	End Time

MEDICATIONS

Time	Name & Dosage

NOTES

NAME: _____ DATE: _____

FEEDING

Time	Breast (Time)	L / R	Bottle (oz.)

DIAPERS

Wet	Dirty
☐	☐
☐	☐
☐	☐
☐	☐
☐	☐
☐	☐
☐	☐
☐	☐

TUMMY TIME

Start Time	End Time

SLEEP/NAPS

Start Time	End Time

MEDICATIONS

Time	Name & Dosage

NOTES

NAME: _____ DATE: _____

FEEDING

Time	Breast (Time) L / R	Bottle (oz.)

DIAPERS

Wet	Dirty
☐	☐
☐	☐
☐	☐
☐	☐
☐	☐
☐	☐
☐	☐
☐	☐

TUMMY TIME

Start Time	End Time

SLEEP/NAPS

Start Time	End Time

MEDICATIONS

Time	Name & Dosage

NOTES

NAME: _____   DATE: _____

FEEDING

Time	Breast (Time)	L / R	Bottle (oz.)

DIAPERS

Wet	Dirty
☐	☐
☐	☐
☐	☐
☐	☐
☐	☐
☐	☐
☐	☐

TUMMY TIME

Start Time	End Time

SLEEP/NAPS

Start Time	End Time

MEDICATIONS

Time	Name & Dosage

NOTES

NAME: _____   DATE: _____

FEEDING

TIME	BREAST (TIME)	L / R	BOTTLE (OZ.)

DIAPERS

WET	DIRTY
☐	☐
☐	☐
☐	☐
☐	☐
☐	☐
☐	☐
☐	☐

TUMMY TIME

START TIME	END TIME

SLEEP/NAPS

START TIME	END TIME

MEDICATIONS

TIME	NAME & DOSAGE

NOTES

NAME: _____ DATE: _____

FEEDING

Time	Breast (Time)	L / R	Bottle (oz.)

DIAPERS

Wet	Dirty
☐	☐
☐	☐
☐	☐
☐	☐
☐	☐
☐	☐
☐	☐
☐	☐

TUMMY TIME

Start Time	End Time

SLEEP/NAPS

Start Time	End Time

MEDICATIONS

Time	Name & Dosage

NOTES

NAME: _____   DATE: _____

FEEDING

Time	Breast (Time) L / R	Bottle (oz.)

DIAPERS

Wet	Dirty
☐	☐
☐	☐
☐	☐
☐	☐
☐	☐
☐	☐
☐	☐
☐	☐

TUMMY TIME

Start Time	End Time

SLEEP/NAPS

Start Time	End Time

MEDICATIONS

Time	Name & Dosage

NOTES

NAME: _____ DATE: _____

FEEDING

Time	Breast (Time)	L / R	Bottle (oz.)

DIAPERS

Wet	Dirty
☐	☐
☐	☐
☐	☐
☐	☐
☐	☐
☐	☐
☐	☐
☐	☐

TUMMY TIME

Start Time	End Time

SLEEP/NAPS

Start Time	End Time

MEDICATIONS

Time	Name & Dosage

NOTES

NAME: _____ DATE: _____

FEEDING

Time	Breast (Time) L / R	Bottle (oz.)

DIAPERS

Wet	Dirty
☐	☐
☐	☐
☐	☐
☐	☐
☐	☐
☐	☐
☐	☐
☐	☐

TUMMY TIME

Start Time	End Time

SLEEP/NAPS

Start Time	End Time

MEDICATIONS

Time	Name & Dosage

NOTES

NAME: _____   DATE: _____

FEEDING

Time	Breast (Time) L / R	Bottle (Oz.)

DIAPERS

Wet	Dirty
☐	☐
☐	☐
☐	☐
☐	☐
☐	☐
☐	☐
☐	☐
☐	☐

TUMMY TIME

Start Time	End Time

SLEEP/NAPS

Start Time	End Time

MEDICATIONS

Time	Name & Dosage

NOTES

NAME: _____   DATE: _____

FEEDING

TIME	BREAST (TIME) L / R	BOTTLE (OZ.)

DIAPERS

WET	DIRTY
☐	☐
☐	☐
☐	☐
☐	☐
☐	☐
☐	☐
☐	☐
☐	☐

TUMMY TIME

START TIME	END TIME

SLEEP/NAPS

START TIME	END TIME

MEDICATIONS

TIME	NAME & DOSAGE

NOTES

NAME: _____   DATE: _____

FEEDING

Time	Breast (Time)	L / R	Bottle (oz.)

DIAPERS

Wet	Dirty
☐	☐
☐	☐
☐	☐
☐	☐
☐	☐
☐	☐
☐	☐

TUMMY TIME

Start Time	End Time

SLEEP/NAPS

Start Time	End Time

MEDICATIONS

Time	Name & Dosage

NOTES

NAME: _____ DATE: _____

FEEDING

Time	Breast (Time)	L / R	Bottle (oz.)

DIAPERS

Wet	Dirty
☐	☐
☐	☐
☐	☐
☐	☐
☐	☐
☐	☐
☐	☐
☐	☐

TUMMY TIME

Start Time	End Time

SLEEP/NAPS

Start Time	End Time

MEDICATIONS

Time	Name & Dosage

NOTES

NAME: _____ DATE: _____

FEEDING

Time	Breast (Time)	L / R	Bottle (oz.)

DIAPERS

Wet	Dirty
☐	☐
☐	☐
☐	☐
☐	☐
☐	☐
☐	☐
☐	☐
☐	☐

TUMMY TIME

Start Time	End Time

SLEEP/NAPS

Start Time	End Time

MEDICATIONS

Time	Name & Dosage

NOTES

NAME: _____   DATE: _____

FEEDING

Time	Breast (Time)	L / R	Bottle (oz.)

DIAPERS

Wet	Dirty
☐	☐
☐	☐
☐	☐
☐	☐
☐	☐
☐	☐
☐	☐
☐	☐

TUMMY TIME

Start Time	End Time

SLEEP/NAPS

Start Time	End Time

MEDICATIONS

Time	Name & Dosage

NOTES

NAME: _____   DATE: _____

FEEDING

Time	Breast (Time)	L / R	Bottle (oz.)

DIAPERS

Wet	Dirty
☐	☐
☐	☐
☐	☐
☐	☐
☐	☐
☐	☐
☐	☐
☐	☐

TUMMY TIME

Start Time	End Time

SLEEP/NAPS

Start Time	End Time

MEDICATIONS

Time	Name & Dosage

NOTES

NAME: _____ DATE: _____

FEEDING

TIME	BREAST (TIME)	L / R	BOTTLE (OZ.)

DIAPERS

WET	DIRTY
☐	☐
☐	☐
☐	☐
☐	☐
☐	☐
☐	☐
☐	☐
☐	☐

TUMMY TIME

START TIME	END TIME

SLEEP/NAPS

START TIME	END TIME

MEDICATIONS

TIME	NAME & DOSAGE

NOTES

NAME: _____ DATE: _____

FEEDING

TIME	BREAST (TIME)	L / R	BOTTLE (OZ.)

DIAPERS

WET	DIRTY
☐	☐
☐	☐
☐	☐
☐	☐
☐	☐
☐	☐
☐	☐
☐	☐

TUMMY TIME

START TIME	END TIME

SLEEP/NAPS

START TIME	END TIME

MEDICATIONS

TIME	NAME & DOSAGE

NOTES

NAME: _____   DATE: _____

FEEDING

TIME	BREAST (TIME)	L / R	BOTTLE (OZ.)

DIAPERS

WET	DIRTY

TUMMY TIME

START TIME	END TIME

SLEEP/NAPS

START TIME	END TIME

MEDICATIONS

TIME	NAME & DOSAGE

NOTES

NAME: _____ DATE: _____

FEEDING

TIME	BREAST (TIME)	L / R	BOTTLE (OZ.)

DIAPERS

WET	DIRTY
☐	☐
☐	☐
☐	☐
☐	☐
☐	☐
☐	☐
☐	☐

TUMMY TIME

START TIME	END TIME

SLEEP/NAPS

START TIME	END TIME

MEDICATIONS

TIME	NAME & DOSAGE

NOTES

NAME: _____   DATE: _____

FEEDING

TIME	BREAST (TIME)	L / R	BOTTLE (OZ.)

DIAPERS

WET	DIRTY

TUMMY TIME

START TIME	END TIME

SLEEP/NAPS

START TIME	END TIME

MEDICATIONS

TIME	NAME & DOSAGE

NOTES

NAME: _____   DATE: _____

FEEDING

Time	Breast (Time)	L / R	Bottle (oz.)

DIAPERS

Wet	Dirty
☐	☐
☐	☐
☐	☐
☐	☐
☐	☐
☐	☐
☐	☐
☐	☐

TUMMY TIME

Start Time	End Time

SLEEP/NAPS

Start Time	End Time

MEDICATIONS

Time	Name & Dosage

NOTES

NAME: _____   DATE: _____

FEEDING

Time	Breast (Time)	L / R	Bottle (oz.)

DIAPERS

Wet	Dirty
☐	☐
☐	☐
☐	☐
☐	☐
☐	☐
☐	☐
☐	☐

TUMMY TIME

Start Time	End Time

SLEEP/NAPS

Start Time	End Time

MEDICATIONS

Time	Name & Dosage

NOTES

Name: _____   Date: _____

FEEDING

Time	Breast (Time)	L / R	Bottle (oz.)

DIAPERS

Wet	Dirty
☐	☐
☐	☐
☐	☐
☐	☐
☐	☐
☐	☐
☐	☐

TUMMY TIME

Start Time	End Time

SLEEP/NAPS

Start Time	End Time

MEDICATIONS

Time	Name & Dosage

NOTES

NAME: _____ DATE: _____

FEEDING

TIME	BREAST (TIME)	L / R	BOTTLE (OZ.)

DIAPERS

WET	DIRTY
☐	☐
☐	☐
☐	☐
☐	☐
☐	☐
☐	☐
☐	☐
☐	☐

TUMMY TIME

START TIME	END TIME

SLEEP/NAPS

START TIME	END TIME

MEDICATIONS

TIME	NAME & DOSAGE

NOTES

NAME: _____ DATE: _____

FEEDING

TIME	BREAST (TIME)	L / R	BOTTLE (OZ.)

DIAPERS

WET	DIRTY
☐	☐
☐	☐
☐	☐
☐	☐
☐	☐
☐	☐
☐	☐
☐	☐

TUMMY TIME

START TIME	END TIME

SLEEP/NAPS

START TIME	END TIME

MEDICATIONS

TIME	NAME & DOSAGE

NOTES

NAME: _____ DATE: _____

FEEDING

TIME	BREAST (TIME)	L / R	BOTTLE (OZ.)

DIAPERS

WET	DIRTY
☐	☐
☐	☐
☐	☐
☐	☐
☐	☐
☐	☐
☐	☐
☐	☐
☐	☐

TUMMY TIME

START TIME	END TIME

SLEEP/NAPS

START TIME	END TIME

MEDICATIONS

TIME	NAME & DOSAGE

NOTES

NAME: _____   DATE: _____

FEEDING

TIME	BREAST (TIME)	L / R	BOTTLE (OZ.)

DIAPERS

WET	DIRTY
☐	☐
☐	☐
☐	☐
☐	☐
☐	☐
☐	☐
☐	☐

TUMMY TIME

START TIME	END TIME

SLEEP/NAPS

START TIME	END TIME

MEDICATIONS

TIME	NAME & DOSAGE

NOTES

NAME: _____ DATE: _____

FEEDING

TIME	BREAST (TIME)	L / R	BOTTLE (OZ.)

DIAPERS

WET	DIRTY

TUMMY TIME

START TIME	END TIME

SLEEP/NAPS

START TIME	END TIME

MEDICATIONS

TIME	NAME & DOSAGE

NOTES

NAME: _____   DATE: _____

FEEDING

TIME	BREAST (TIME)	L / R	BOTTLE (OZ.)

DIAPERS

WET	DIRTY
☐	☐
☐	☐
☐	☐
☐	☐
☐	☐
☐	☐
☐	☐

TUMMY TIME

START TIME	END TIME

SLEEP/NAPS

START TIME	END TIME

MEDICATIONS

TIME	NAME & DOSAGE

NOTES

NAME: _____ DATE: _____

FEEDING

TIME	BREAST (TIME)	L / R	BOTTLE (OZ.)

DIAPERS

WET	DIRTY

TUMMY TIME

START TIME	END TIME

SLEEP/NAPS

START TIME	END TIME

MEDICATIONS

TIME	NAME & DOSAGE

NOTES

NAME: _____   DATE: _____

FEEDING

Time	Breast (Time)	L / R	Bottle (oz.)

DIAPERS

Wet	Dirty
☐	☐
☐	☐
☐	☐
☐	☐
☐	☐
☐	☐
☐	☐
☐	☐

TUMMY TIME

Start Time	End Time

SLEEP/NAPS

Start Time	End Time

MEDICATIONS

Time	Name & Dosage

NOTES

NAME: _____   DATE: _____

FEEDING

TIME	BREAST (TIME)	L / R	BOTTLE (OZ.)

DIAPERS

WET	DIRTY

TUMMY TIME

START TIME	END TIME

SLEEP/NAPS

START TIME	END TIME

MEDICATIONS

TIME	NAME & DOSAGE

NOTES

NAME: _____   DATE: _____

FEEDING

Time	Breast (Time)	L / R	Bottle (oz.)

DIAPERS

Wet	Dirty
☐	☐
☐	☐
☐	☐
☐	☐
☐	☐
☐	☐
☐	☐
☐	☐

TUMMY TIME

Start Time	End Time

SLEEP/NAPS

Start Time	End Time

MEDICATIONS

Time	Name & Dosage

NOTES

NAME: _____   DATE: _____

FEEDING

Time	Breast (Time)	L / R	Bottle (oz.)

DIAPERS

Wet	Dirty
☐	☐
☐	☐
☐	☐
☐	☐
☐	☐
☐	☐
☐	☐
☐	☐

TUMMY TIME

Start Time	End Time

SLEEP/NAPS

Start Time	End Time

MEDICATIONS

Time	Name & Dosage

NOTES

NAME: _____ DATE: _____

FEEDING

TIME	BREAST (TIME)	L / R	BOTTLE (OZ.)

DIAPERS

WET	DIRTY
☐	☐
☐	☐
☐	☐
☐	☐
☐	☐
☐	☐
☐	☐

TUMMY TIME

START TIME	END TIME

SLEEP/NAPS

START TIME	END TIME

MEDICATIONS

TIME	NAME & DOSAGE

NOTES

NAME: _____   DATE: _____

FEEDING

TIME	BREAST (TIME)	L / R	BOTTLE (OZ.)

DIAPERS

WET	DIRTY

TUMMY TIME

START TIME	END TIME

SLEEP/NAPS

START TIME	END TIME

MEDICATIONS

TIME	NAME & DOSAGE

NOTES

NAME: _____   DATE: _____

FEEDING

Time	Breast (Time)	L / R	Bottle (oz.)

DIAPERS

Wet	Dirty
☐	☐
☐	☐
☐	☐
☐	☐
☐	☐
☐	☐
☐	☐
☐	☐

TUMMY TIME

Start Time	End Time

SLEEP/NAPS

Start Time	End Time

MEDICATIONS

Time	Name & Dosage

NOTES

NAME: _____   DATE: _____

FEEDING

Time	Breast (Time)	L / R	Bottle (oz.)

DIAPERS

Wet	Dirty
☐	☐
☐	☐
☐	☐
☐	☐
☐	☐
☐	☐
☐	☐
☐	☐

TUMMY TIME

Start Time	End Time

SLEEP/NAPS

Start Time	End Time

MEDICATIONS

Time	Name & Dosage

NOTES

NAME: _____ DATE: _____

FEEDING

Time	Breast (Time)	L / R	Bottle (oz.)

DIAPERS

Wet	Dirty
☐	☐
☐	☐
☐	☐
☐	☐
☐	☐
☐	☐
☐	☐
☐	☐

TUMMY TIME

Start Time	End Time

SLEEP/NAPS

Start Time	End Time

MEDICATIONS

Time	Name & Dosage

NOTES

NAME: _____ DATE: _____

FEEDING

Time	Breast (Time)	L / R	Bottle (oz.)

DIAPERS

Wet	Dirty
☐	☐
☐	☐
☐	☐
☐	☐
☐	☐
☐	☐
☐	☐
☐	☐

TUMMY TIME

Start Time	End Time

SLEEP/NAPS

Start Time	End Time

MEDICATIONS

Time	Name & Dosage

NOTES

NAME: _____   DATE: _____

FEEDING

TIME	BREAST (TIME)	L / R	BOTTLE (OZ.)

DIAPERS

WET	DIRTY
☐	☐
☐	☐
☐	☐
☐	☐
☐	☐
☐	☐
☐	☐
☐	☐

TUMMY TIME

START TIME	END TIME

SLEEP/NAPS

START TIME	END TIME

MEDICATIONS

TIME	NAME & DOSAGE

NOTES

NAME: _____ DATE: _____

FEEDING

Time	Breast (Time)	L / R	Bottle (oz.)

DIAPERS

Wet	Dirty

TUMMY TIME

Start Time	End Time

SLEEP/NAPS

Start Time	End Time

MEDICATIONS

Time	Name & Dosage

NOTES

Name: _____ Date: _____

FEEDING

Time	Breast (Time)	L / R	Bottle (Oz.)

DIAPERS

Wet	Dirty
☐	☐
☐	☐
☐	☐
☐	☐
☐	☐
☐	☐
☐	☐
	☐

TUMMY TIME

Start Time	End Time

SLEEP/NAPS

Start Time	End Time

MEDICATIONS

Time	Name & Dosage

NOTES

NAME: _____   DATE: _____

FEEDING

Time	Breast (Time)	L / R	Bottle (oz.)

DIAPERS

Wet	Dirty
☐	☐
☐	☐
☐	☐
☐	☐
☐	☐
☐	☐
☐	☐
☐	☐

TUMMY TIME

Start Time	End Time

SLEEP/NAPS

Start Time	End Time

MEDICATIONS

Time	Name & Dosage

NOTES

Name: _____   Date: _____

FEEDING

Time	Breast (Time)	L / R	Bottle (oz.)

DIAPERS

Wet	Dirty
☐	☐
☐	☐
☐	☐
☐	☐
☐	☐
☐	☐
☐	☐

TUMMY TIME

Start Time	End Time

SLEEP/NAPS

Start Time	End Time

MEDICATIONS

Time	Name & Dosage

NOTES

NAME: _____   DATE: _____

FEEDING

TIME	BREAST (TIME)	L / R	BOTTLE (OZ.)

DIAPERS

WET	DIRTY
☐	☐
☐	☐
☐	☐
☐	☐
☐	☐
☐	☐
☐	☐
☐	☐

TUMMY TIME

START TIME	END TIME

SLEEP/NAPS

START TIME	END TIME

MEDICATIONS

TIME	NAME & DOSAGE

NOTES

Name: _____ Date: _____

FEEDING

Time	Breast (Time)	L / R	Bottle (oz.)

DIAPERS

Wet	Dirty
☐	☐
☐	☐
☐	☐
☐	☐
☐	☐
☐	☐
☐	☐
☐	☐

TUMMY TIME

Start Time	End Time

SLEEP/NAPS

Start Time	End Time

MEDICATIONS

Time	Name & Dosage

NOTES

NAME: _____   DATE: _____

FEEDING

TIME	BREAST (TIME)	L / R	BOTTLE (OZ.)

DIAPERS

WET	DIRTY

TUMMY TIME

START TIME	END TIME

SLEEP/NAPS

START TIME	END TIME

MEDICATIONS

TIME	NAME & DOSAGE

NOTES

NAME: _____   DATE: _____

FEEDING

TIME	BREAST (TIME) L / R	BOTTLE (OZ.)

DIAPERS

WET	DIRTY
☐	☐
☐	☐
☐	☐
☐	☐
☐	☐
☐	☐
☐	☐
☐	☐

TUMMY TIME

START TIME	END TIME

SLEEP/NAPS

START TIME	END TIME

MEDICATIONS

TIME	NAME & DOSAGE

NOTES

NAME: _____ DATE: _____

FEEDING

TIME	BREAST (TIME)	L / R	BOTTLE (OZ.)

DIAPERS

WET	DIRTY
☐	☐
☐	☐
☐	☐
☐	☐
☐	☐
☐	☐
☐	☐
☐	☐

TUMMY TIME

START TIME	END TIME

SLEEP/NAPS

START TIME	END TIME

MEDICATIONS

TIME	NAME & DOSAGE

NOTES

NAME: _____   DATE: _____

FEEDING

TIME	BREAST (TIME)	L / R	BOTTLE (OZ.)

DIAPERS

WET	DIRTY

TUMMY TIME

START TIME	END TIME

SLEEP/NAPS

START TIME	END TIME

MEDICATIONS

TIME	NAME & DOSAGE

NOTES

NAME: _____   DATE: _____

FEEDING

TIME	BREAST (TIME)	L / R	BOTTLE (OZ.)

DIAPERS

WET	DIRTY
☐	☐
☐	☐
☐	☐
☐	☐
☐	☐
☐	☐
☐	☐
☐	☐

TUMMY TIME

START TIME	END TIME

SLEEP/NAPS

START TIME	END TIME

MEDICATIONS

TIME	NAME & DOSAGE

NOTES

NAME: _____   DATE: _____

FEEDING

TIME	BREAST (TIME)	L / R	BOTTLE (OZ.)

DIAPERS

WET	DIRTY
☐	☐
☐	☐
☐	☐
☐	☐
☐	☐
☐	☐
☐	☐

TUMMY TIME

START TIME	END TIME

SLEEP/NAPS

START TIME	END TIME

MEDICATIONS

TIME	NAME & DOSAGE

NOTES

NAME: _____   DATE: _____

FEEDING

TIME	BREAST (TIME)	L / R	BOTTLE (OZ.)

DIAPERS

WET	DIRTY
☐	☐
☐	☐
☐	☐
☐	☐
☐	☐
☐	☐
☐	☐
☐	☐

TUMMY TIME

START TIME	END TIME

SLEEP/NAPS

START TIME	END TIME

MEDICATIONS

TIME	NAME & DOSAGE

NOTES

NAME: _____   DATE: _____

FEEDING

Time	Breast (Time)	L / R	Bottle (oz.)

DIAPERS

Wet	Dirty
☐	☐
☐	☐
☐	☐
☐	☐
☐	☐
☐	☐
☐	☐
☐	☐

TUMMY TIME

Start Time	End Time

SLEEP/NAPS

Start Time	End Time

MEDICATIONS

Time	Name & Dosage

NOTES

NAME: _____   DATE: _____

FEEDING

TIME	BREAST (TIME)	L / R	BOTTLE (OZ.)

DIAPERS

WET	DIRTY
☐	☐
☐	☐
☐	☐
☐	☐
☐	☐
☐	☐
☐	☐
☐	☐

TUMMY TIME

START TIME	END TIME

SLEEP/NAPS

START TIME	END TIME

MEDICATIONS

TIME	NAME & DOSAGE

NOTES

NAME: _____   DATE: _____

FEEDING

TIME	BREAST (TIME)	L / R	BOTTLE (OZ.)

DIAPERS

WET	DIRTY
☐	☐
☐	☐
☐	☐
☐	☐
☐	☐
☐	☐
☐	☐
☐	☐

TUMMY TIME

START TIME	END TIME

SLEEP/NAPS

START TIME	END TIME

MEDICATIONS

TIME	NAME & DOSAGE

NOTES

NAME: _____   DATE: _____

FEEDING

TIME	BREAST (TIME)	L / R	BOTTLE (OZ.)

DIAPERS

WET	DIRTY
☐	☐
☐	☐
☐	☐
☐	☐
☐	☐
☐	☐
☐	☐
☐	☐

TUMMY TIME

START TIME	END TIME

SLEEP/NAPS

START TIME	END TIME

MEDICATIONS

TIME	NAME & DOSAGE

NOTES

NAME: _____   DATE: _____

FEEDING

Time	Breast (Time)	L / R	Bottle (oz.)

DIAPERS

Wet	Dirty
☐	☐
☐	☐
☐	☐
☐	☐
☐	☐
☐	☐
☐	☐
☐	☐

TUMMY TIME

Start Time	End Time

SLEEP/NAPS

Start Time	End Time

MEDICATIONS

Time	Name & Dosage

NOTES

NAME: _____   DATE: _____

FEEDING

TIME	BREAST (TIME)	L / R	BOTTLE (OZ.)

DIAPERS

WET	DIRTY
☐	☐
☐	☐
☐	☐
☐	☐
☐	☐
☐	☐
☐	☐
☐	☐

TUMMY TIME

START TIME	END TIME

SLEEP/NAPS

START TIME	END TIME

MEDICATIONS

TIME	NAME & DOSAGE

NOTES

Name: _____   Date: _____

FEEDING

Time	Breast (Time)	L / R	Bottle (oz.)

DIAPERS

Wet	Dirty
☐	☐
☐	☐
☐	☐
☐	☐
☐	☐
☐	☐
☐	☐
☐	☐

TUMMY TIME

Start Time	End Time

SLEEP/NAPS

Start Time	End Time

MEDICATIONS

Time	Name & Dosage

NOTES

NAME: _____   DATE: _____

FEEDING

Time	Breast (Time)	L / R	Bottle (Oz.)

DIAPERS

Wet	Dirty
☐	☐
☐	☐
☐	☐
☐	☐
☐	☐
☐	☐
☐	☐
☐	☐

TUMMY TIME

Start Time	End Time

SLEEP/NAPS

Start Time	End Time

MEDICATIONS

Time	Name & Dosage

NOTES

NAME: _____   DATE: _____

FEEDING

TIME	BREAST (TIME)	L / R	BOTTLE (OZ.)

DIAPERS

WET	DIRTY
☐	☐
☐	☐
☐	☐
☐	☐
☐	☐
☐	☐
☐	☐

TUMMY TIME

START TIME	END TIME

SLEEP/NAPS

START TIME	END TIME

MEDICATIONS

TIME	NAME & DOSAGE

NOTES

NAME: _____ DATE: _____

FEEDING

TIME	BREAST (TIME)	L / R	BOTTLE (OZ.)

DIAPERS

WET	DIRTY
☐	☐
☐	☐
☐	☐
☐	☐
☐	☐
☐	☐
☐	☐
☐	☐

TUMMY TIME

START TIME	END TIME

SLEEP/NAPS

START TIME	END TIME

MEDICATIONS

TIME	NAME & DOSAGE

NOTES

Name: _____   Date: _____

FEEDING

Time	Breast (Time)	L / R	Bottle (oz.)

DIAPERS

Wet	Dirty
☐	☐
☐	☐
☐	☐
☐	☐
☐	☐
☐	☐
☐	☐
☐	☐

TUMMY TIME

Start Time	End Time

SLEEP/NAPS

Start Time	End Time

MEDICATIONS

Time	Name & Dosage

NOTES

NAME: _____   DATE: _____

FEEDING

TIME	BREAST (TIME)	L / R	BOTTLE (OZ.)

DIAPERS

WET	DIRTY

TUMMY TIME

START TIME	END TIME

SLEEP/NAPS

START TIME	END TIME

MEDICATIONS

TIME	NAME & DOSAGE

NOTES

NAME: _____   DATE: _____

FEEDING

Time	Breast (Time)	L / R	Bottle (oz.)

DIAPERS

Wet	Dirty
☐	☐
☐	☐
☐	☐
☐	☐
☐	☐
☐	☐
☐	☐
☐	☐

TUMMY TIME

Start Time	End Time

SLEEP/NAPS

Start Time	End Time

MEDICATIONS

Time	Name & Dosage

NOTES

NAME: _____   DATE: _____

FEEDING

TIME	BREAST (TIME)	L / R	BOTTLE (OZ.)

DIAPERS

WET	DIRTY
☐	☐
☐	☐
☐	☐
☐	☐
☐	☐
☐	☐
☐	☐
☐	☐

TUMMY TIME

START TIME	END TIME

SLEEP/NAPS

START TIME	END TIME

MEDICATIONS

TIME	NAME & DOSAGE

NOTES

NAME: _____   DATE: _____

FEEDING

Time	Breast (Time)	L / R	Bottle (oz.)

DIAPERS

Wet	Dirty
☐	☐
☐	☐
☐	☐
☐	☐
☐	☐
☐	☐
☐	☐
☐	☐

TUMMY TIME

Start Time	End Time

SLEEP/NAPS

Start Time	End Time

MEDICATIONS

Time	Name & Dosage

NOTES

NAME: _____ DATE: _____

FEEDING

Time	Breast (Time)	L / R	Bottle (oz.)

DIAPERS

Wet	Dirty
☐	☐
☐	☐
☐	☐
☐	☐
☐	☐
☐	☐
☐	☐
☐	☐

TUMMY TIME

Start Time	End Time

SLEEP/NAPS

Start Time	End Time

MEDICATIONS

Time	Name & Dosage

NOTES

NAME: _____ DATE: _____

FEEDING

Time	Breast (Time)	L / R	Bottle (oz.)

DIAPERS

Wet	Dirty
☐	☐
☐	☐
☐	☐
☐	☐
☐	☐
☐	☐
☐	

TUMMY TIME

Start Time	End Time

SLEEP/NAPS

Start Time	End Time

MEDICATIONS

Time	Name & Dosage

NOTES

NAME: _____   DATE: _____

FEEDING

TIME	BREAST (TIME)	L / R	BOTTLE (OZ.)

DIAPERS

WET	DIRTY
☐	☐
☐	☐
☐	☐
☐	☐
☐	☐
☐	☐
☐	☐
☐	☐

TUMMY TIME

START TIME	END TIME

SLEEP/NAPS

START TIME	END TIME

MEDICATIONS

TIME	NAME & DOSAGE

NOTES

NAME: _____   DATE: _____

FEEDING

TIME	BREAST (TIME) L / R	BOTTLE (OZ.)

DIAPERS

WET	DIRTY
☐	☐
☐	☐
☐	☐
☐	☐
☐	☐
☐	☐
☐	☐
☐	☐

TUMMY TIME

START TIME	END TIME

SLEEP/NAPS

START TIME	END TIME

MEDICATIONS

TIME	NAME & DOSAGE

NOTES

NAME: _____   DATE: _____

FEEDING

TIME	BREAST (TIME)	L / R	BOTTLE (OZ.)

DIAPERS

WET	DIRTY
☐	☐
☐	☐
☐	☐
☐	☐
☐	☐
☐	☐
☐	☐
☐	☐

TUMMY TIME

START TIME	END TIME

SLEEP/NAPS

START TIME	END TIME

MEDICATIONS

TIME	NAME & DOSAGE

NOTES

NAME: _____ DATE: _____

FEEDING

Time	Breast (Time)	L / R	Bottle (oz.)

DIAPERS

Wet	Dirty
☐	☐
☐	☐
☐	☐
☐	☐
☐	☐
☐	☐
☐	☐

TUMMY TIME

Start Time	End Time

SLEEP/NAPS

Start Time	End Time

MEDICATIONS

Time	Name & Dosage

NOTES

NAME: _____   DATE: _____

FEEDING

Time	Breast (Time)	L / R	Bottle (oz.)

DIAPERS

Wet	Dirty
☐	☐
☐	☐
☐	☐
☐	☐
☐	☐
☐	☐
☐	☐
☐	☐

TUMMY TIME

Start Time	End Time

SLEEP/NAPS

Start Time	End Time

MEDICATIONS

Time	Name & Dosage

NOTES

NAME: _____   DATE: _____

FEEDING

Time	Breast (Time)	L / R	Bottle (oz.)

DIAPERS

Wet	Dirty
☐	☐
☐	☐
☐	☐
☐	☐
☐	☐
☐	☐
☐	☐
☐	☐

TUMMY TIME

Start Time	End Time

SLEEP/NAPS

Start Time	End Time

MEDICATIONS

Time	Name & Dosage

NOTES

NAME: _____   DATE: _____

FEEDING

TIME	BREAST (TIME)	L / R	BOTTLE (OZ.)

DIAPERS

WET	DIRTY

TUMMY TIME

START TIME	END TIME

SLEEP/NAPS

START TIME	END TIME

MEDICATIONS

TIME	NAME & DOSAGE

NOTES

NAME: _____   DATE: _____

FEEDING

TIME	BREAST (TIME) L/R	BOTTLE (OZ.)

DIAPERS

WET	DIRTY

TUMMY TIME

START TIME	END TIME

SLEEP/NAPS

START TIME	END TIME

MEDICATIONS

TIME	NAME & DOSAGE

NOTES

NAME: _____ DATE: _____

FEEDING

Time	Breast (Time)	L / R	Bottle (oz.)

DIAPERS

Wet	Dirty

TUMMY TIME

Start Time	End Time

SLEEP/NAPS

Start Time	End Time

MEDICATIONS

Time	Name & Dosage

NOTES

NAME: _____   DATE: _____

FEEDING

TIME	BREAST (TIME)	L / R	BOTTLE (OZ.)

DIAPERS

WET	DIRTY

TUMMY TIME

START TIME	END TIME

SLEEP/NAPS

START TIME	END TIME

MEDICATIONS

TIME	NAME & DOSAGE

NOTES

NAME: _____ DATE: _____

FEEDING

TIME	BREAST (TIME)	L / R	BOTTLE (OZ.)

DIAPERS

WET	DIRTY
☐	☐
☐	☐
☐	☐
☐	☐
☐	☐
☐	☐
☐	☐
☐	☐

TUMMY TIME

START TIME	END TIME

SLEEP/NAPS

START TIME	END TIME

MEDICATIONS

TIME	NAME & DOSAGE

NOTES

NAME: _____ DATE: _____

FEEDING

TIME	BREAST (TIME)	L / R	BOTTLE (OZ.)

DIAPERS

WET	DIRTY
☐	☐
☐	☐
☐	☐
☐	☐
☐	☐
☐	☐
☐	☐
☐	☐

TUMMY TIME

START TIME	END TIME

SLEEP/NAPS

START TIME	END TIME

MEDICATIONS

TIME	NAME & DOSAGE

NOTES

NAME: _____   DATE: _____

FEEDING

TIME	BREAST (TIME)	L / R	BOTTLE (OZ.)

DIAPERS

WET	DIRTY

TUMMY TIME

START TIME	END TIME

SLEEP/NAPS

START TIME	END TIME

MEDICATIONS

TIME	NAME & DOSAGE

NOTES

NAME: _____   DATE: _____

FEEDING

Time	Breast (Time)	L / R	Bottle (Oz.)

DIAPERS

Wet	Dirty
☐	☐
☐	☐
☐	☐
☐	☐
☐	☐
☐	☐
☐	☐
☐	☐

TUMMY TIME

Start Time	End Time

SLEEP/NAPS

Start Time	End Time

MEDICATIONS

Time	Name & Dosage

NOTES

NAME: _____   DATE: _____

FEEDING

Time	Breast (Time)	L / R	Bottle (oz.)

DIAPERS

Wet	Dirty
☐	☐
☐	☐
☐	☐
☐	☐
☐	☐
☐	☐
☐	☐
☐	☐

TUMMY TIME

Start Time	End Time

SLEEP/NAPS

Start Time	End Time

MEDICATIONS

Time	Name & Dosage

NOTES

NAME: _____ DATE: _____

FEEDING

Time	Breast (Time)	L / R	Bottle (oz.)

DIAPERS

Wet	Dirty
☐	☐
☐	☐
☐	☐
☐	☐
☐	☐
☐	☐
☐	☐
☐	☐

TUMMY TIME

Start Time	End Time

SLEEP/NAPS

Start Time	End Time

MEDICATIONS

Time	Name & Dosage

NOTES

NAME: _____   DATE: _____

FEEDING

TIME	BREAST (TIME)	L / R	BOTTLE (OZ.)

DIAPERS

WET	DIRTY

TUMMY TIME

START TIME	END TIME

SLEEP/NAPS

START TIME	END TIME

MEDICATIONS

TIME	NAME & DOSAGE

NOTES

NAME: _____ DATE: _____

FEEDING

TIME	BREAST (TIME)	L / R	BOTTLE (OZ.)

DIAPERS

WET	DIRTY
☐	☐
☐	☐
☐	☐
☐	☐
☐	☐
☐	☐
☐	☐

TUMMY TIME

START TIME	END TIME

SLEEP/NAPS

START TIME	END TIME

MEDICATIONS

TIME	NAME & DOSAGE

NOTES

NAME: _____   DATE: _____

FEEDING

TIME	BREAST (TIME)	L / R	BOTTLE (OZ.)

DIAPERS

WET	DIRTY
☐	☐
☐	☐
☐	☐
☐	☐
☐	☐
☐	☐
☐	☐

TUMMY TIME

START TIME	END TIME

SLEEP/NAPS

START TIME	END TIME

MEDICATIONS

TIME	NAME & DOSAGE

NOTES

NAME: _____   DATE: _____

FEEDING

TIME	BREAST (TIME)	L / R	BOTTLE (OZ.)

DIAPERS

WET	DIRTY
☐	☐
☐	☐
☐	☐
☐	☐
☐	☐
☐	☐
☐	

TUMMY TIME

START TIME	END TIME

SLEEP/NAPS

START TIME	END TIME

MEDICATIONS

TIME	NAME & DOSAGE

NOTES

NAME: _____   DATE: _____

FEEDING

Time	Breast (Time) L / R	Bottle (Oz.)

DIAPERS

Wet	Dirty
☐	☐
☐	☐
☐	☐
☐	☐
☐	☐
☐	☐
☐	☐
☐	☐

TUMMY TIME

Start Time	End Time

SLEEP/NAPS

Start Time	End Time

MEDICATIONS

Time	Name & Dosage

NOTES

Name: _____ Date: _____

FEEDING

Time	Breast (Time)	L / R	Bottle (oz.)

DIAPERS

Wet	Dirty
☐	☐
☐	☐
☐	☐
☐	☐
☐	☐
☐	☐
☐	☐

TUMMY TIME

Start Time	End Time

SLEEP/NAPS

Start Time	End Time

MEDICATIONS

Time	Name & Dosage

NOTES

NAME: _____ DATE: _____

FEEDING

TIME	BREAST (TIME)	L / R	BOTTLE (OZ.)

DIAPERS

WET	DIRTY

TUMMY TIME

START TIME	END TIME

SLEEP/NAPS

START TIME	END TIME

MEDICATIONS

TIME	NAME & DOSAGE

NOTES

Name: _____   Date: _____

FEEDING

Time	Breast (Time)	L / R	Bottle (oz.)

DIAPERS

Wet	Dirty
☐	☐
☐	☐
☐	☐
☐	☐
☐	☐
☐	☐
☐	☐

TUMMY TIME

Start Time	End Time

SLEEP/NAPS

Start Time	End Time

MEDICATIONS

Time	Name & Dosage

NOTES

NAME: _____   DATE: _____

FEEDING

Time	Breast (Time)	L / R	Bottle (oz.)

DIAPERS

Wet	Dirty
☐	☐
☐	☐
☐	☐
☐	☐
☐	☐
☐	☐
☐	☐
☐	☐

TUMMY TIME

Start Time	End Time

SLEEP/NAPS

Start Time	End Time

MEDICATIONS

Time	Name & Dosage

NOTES

NAME: _____   DATE: _____

FEEDING

TIME	BREAST (TIME)	L / R	BOTTLE (OZ.)

DIAPERS

WET	DIRTY

TUMMY TIME

START TIME	END TIME

SLEEP/NAPS

START TIME	END TIME

MEDICATIONS

TIME	NAME & DOSAGE

NOTES

NAME: _____   DATE: _____

FEEDING

TIME	BREAST (TIME)	L / R	BOTTLE (OZ.)

DIAPERS

WET	DIRTY
☐	☐
☐	☐
☐	☐
☐	☐
☐	☐
☐	☐
☐	☐
☐	☐

TUMMY TIME

START TIME	END TIME

SLEEP/NAPS

START TIME	END TIME

MEDICATIONS

TIME	NAME & DOSAGE

NOTES

NAME: _____   DATE: _____

FEEDING

TIME	BREAST (TIME)	L / R	BOTTLE (OZ.)

DIAPERS

WET	DIRTY
☐	☐
☐	☐
☐	☐
☐	☐
☐	☐
☐	☐
☐	☐
☐	☐

TUMMY TIME

START TIME	END TIME

SLEEP/NAPS

START TIME	END TIME

MEDICATIONS

TIME	NAME & DOSAGE

NOTES

NAME: _____   DATE: _____

FEEDING

Time	Breast (Time)	L / R	Bottle (oz.)

DIAPERS

Wet	Dirty
☐	☐
☐	☐
☐	☐
☐	☐
☐	☐
☐	☐
☐	☐
☐	☐

TUMMY TIME

Start Time	End Time

SLEEP/NAPS

Start Time	End Time

MEDICATIONS

Time	Name & Dosage

NOTES

NAME: _____ DATE: _____

FEEDING

Time	Breast (Time)	L / R	Bottle (oz.)

DIAPERS

Wet	Dirty
☐	☐
☐	☐
☐	☐
☐	☐
☐	☐
☐	☐
☐	☐
☐	☐

TUMMY TIME

Start Time	End Time

SLEEP/NAPS

Start Time	End Time

MEDICATIONS

Time	Name & Dosage

NOTES

NAME: _____   DATE: _____

FEEDING

TIME	BREAST (TIME) L / R	BOTTLE (OZ.)

DIAPERS

WET	DIRTY
☐	☐
☐	☐
☐	☐
☐	☐
☐	☐
☐	☐
☐	☐
☐	☐

TUMMY TIME

START TIME	END TIME

SLEEP/NAPS

START TIME	END TIME

MEDICATIONS

TIME	NAME & DOSAGE

NOTES

NAME: _____   DATE: _____

FEEDING

Time	Breast (Time)	L / R	Bottle (oz.)

DIAPERS

Wet	Dirty
☐	☐
☐	☐
☐	☐
☐	☐
☐	☐
☐	☐
☐	☐
☐	☐

TUMMY TIME

Start Time	End Time

SLEEP/NAPS

Start Time	End Time

MEDICATIONS

Time	Name & Dosage

NOTES

NAME: _____   DATE: _____

FEEDING

TIME	BREAST (TIME)	L / R	BOTTLE (OZ.)

DIAPERS

WET	DIRTY

TUMMY TIME

START TIME	END TIME

SLEEP/NAPS

START TIME	END TIME

MEDICATIONS

TIME	NAME & DOSAGE

NOTES

NAME: _____   DATE: _____

FEEDING

Time	Breast (Time)	L / R	Bottle (oz.)

DIAPERS

Wet	Dirty
☐	☐
☐	☐
☐	☐
☐	☐
☐	☐
☐	☐
☐	☐
☐	☐

TUMMY TIME

Start Time	End Time

SLEEP/NAPS

Start Time	End Time

MEDICATIONS

Time	Name & Dosage

NOTES

NAME: _____   DATE: _____

FEEDING

TIME	BREAST (TIME) L / R	BOTTLE (OZ.)

DIAPERS

WET	DIRTY
☐	☐
☐	☐
☐	☐
☐	☐
☐	☐
☐	☐
☐	☐
☐	

TUMMY TIME

START TIME	END TIME

SLEEP/NAPS

START TIME	END TIME

MEDICATIONS

TIME	NAME & DOSAGE

NOTES

NAME: _____   DATE: _____

FEEDING

Time	Breast (Time)	L / R	Bottle (oz.)

DIAPERS

Wet	Dirty
☐	☐
☐	☐
☐	☐
☐	☐
☐	☐
☐	☐
☐	☐
☐	☐

TUMMY TIME

Start Time	End Time

SLEEP/NAPS

Start Time	End Time

MEDICATIONS

Time	Name & Dosage

NOTES

Made in the USA
Middletown, DE
29 January 2023